Original title:
The Water's Whisper

Copyright © 2025 Creative Arts Management OÜ
All rights reserved.

Author: Nora Sinclair
ISBN HARDBACK: 978-1-80581-641-6
ISBN PAPERBACK: 978-1-80581-168-8
ISBN EBOOK: 978-1-80581-641-6

Murmuring Shallows

In shallow pools where fish do glide,
The frogs wear crowns, their royal pride.
They croak their jokes with such a flair,
As bubbles rise, they hide in air.

The clumsy ducks, with waddles wide,
Do dance with rhythm, bonny-eyed.
They slip and flop, a silly sight,
As splashes quack, both day and night.

Currents of Time

Oh time flows by, like dodgy streams,
With fish that speak, or so it seems.
They laugh at days, and poke at years,
In silly glee, dismissing fears.

The turtles boast of wisdom's game,
While doing laps, they take their aim.
But somehow I defeat them all,
As I just sit and watch them crawl.

Eddies of Emotion

In twists and turns, the giggles churn,
The stream's own heart, where feelings learn.
With ripples wide, joy bounces back,
But trouble brews—it's time to quack!

The minnows spin with wild delight,
While grumpy crabs just want to fight.
But laughter tames, and ebbing flows,
Make grumpy crabs quite soft like dough.

Shimmering Secrets

In glistening depths, where secrets hide,
The little minnows play and glide.
With whispers shared, they plot and scheme,
To outsmart all in their fishy dream.

The snappy snaps, with sneaky grace,
In wiggly dance, they take their place.
But oops! They trip; oh what a splash!
As laughter echoes, in goofy rash.

Reflections on a Silver Surface

In the pond, a frog leaps high,
Splashing droplets that say hi.
A fish swims by with quite a grin,
"I thought you'd never let me in!"

The sun above starts to bake,
While ducks dive in for a quick shake.
They quack and splash, what a delight,
Making waves and laughing bright!

Dance of the Raindrops

As raindrops fall, the puddles grow,
A tiny frog found quite a show.
With jumps and spins, he took the lead,
Who knew the rain could fuel such speed?

Umbrellas bob like dancing hats,
While kids splash in the charts of splats.
Each drop a laugh, a jig, a cheer,
Who knew the storm could bring such cheer?

Fluid Dreams

A river dreams of being seas,
While fish play tag among the leaves.
"No currents here!" the minnows sigh,
As frogs leap up to kiss the sky.

A turtle snickers, taking his time,
"These dreams of waves are quite a climb!"
But with a wink, he joins the race,
A slowpoke's charm, a smiling face!

Tales of the Riverbed

On a riverbed, a story's spun,
Of pebbles dancing just for fun.
A snail narrates with wiggly flair,
As ants march past without a care.

Each ripple tells a joke or two,
How fish enjoy a bubble brew.
With gurgles loud and splashes loud,
The river chuckles, oh so proud!

Chants of the Celestial Current

In rivers bright, the fish do dance,
With fins that twirl, they take a chance.
They giggle as they swim around,
A splash of joy is all they've found.

The turtles wear their silly hats,
While frogs join in like jumping mats.
A chorus sings in bubbly rhyme,
They laugh at life, it's swimming time!

Melodies of the Calm Shore

Seagulls squawk with utmost flair,
While crabs in suits just do not care.
They shuffle sideways, no big fuss,
In this odd show, we ride the bus.

The waves will clap with gentle cheers,
As shells play hide and seek, it's clear.
Sandy toes and sunny smiles,
Together we have loads of wiles.

Hidden Currents of Silent Truth

The brook is bubbling with a jest,
It tells the rocks just how to rest.
With secret smiles, it shares its tale,
Of rubber ducks that brave the gale.

The otters glide in slippery lines,
They share their snacks and laugh in signs.
"Who needs a map?" one boldly croaks,
When drifting on in muddy strokes.

The Soft Caress of Rivers

The playful splash makes fish look spry,
While turtles giggle 'What a lie!'
But just a wink from passing ducks,
Turns all the frowns to happy plucks.

The river banks with jokes abound,
A splash of humor all around.
So come on down and feel the fun,
In funny waters, everyone!

Trinkets of the Tide

Shells dance in the foam,
Like hats on a crab's dome.
A starfish shows its flair,
Waving like it just don't care.

Seagulls play a sneaky game,
Stealing chips, oh what a shame!
The beach ball rolls with glee,
Chasing after me, oh wee!

Illuminated Ripples

Bubbles tickle my toes,
As fish sing their rhyming prose.
A dolphin dives in for a laugh,
Wearing a seaweed scarf, oh chaff!

The sun paints stripes on a whale,
Who dances like a floppy tail.
Each wave's a playful tease,
Tickling undersea knees.

Whispers of the Reef

An octopus plays peek-a-boo,
With colors bright, a crafty view.
Seahorses twirl, a waltzing show,
With tiny shoes that don't quite glow.

Coral giggles in the breeze,
Tickling fish, such a tease!
They splash and swirl in joyful plight,
Turning dusk into daylight.

Ephemeral Waters

A crab juggles seashells with flair,
While a clam plays dentist with a stare.
The turtles compete in a slow-motion race,
Trying their best to keep pace.

Waves make funny faces as they crest,
A clam in a tux, looking its best.
Each glint and glimmer, a shout of glee,
In the tide's silly jubilee.

Ripples of Serenity

In a pond where frogs do leap,
The fish below have secrets deep.
With every splash, they share a joke,
While ducks quack tales of silly yoke.

A turtle sunbathes, all relaxed,
While catfish ponder, quite un-taxed.
As lily pads hold dance parties grand,
The dragonflies play their little band.

Echoes Beneath the Surface

In the depths, the minnows play,
While eels go 'round in a wiggly ballet.
The bubbles giggle, pop and tease,
As shrimp do cha-cha with the sea breeze.

A crab in boots dances with flair,
While seaweed sways without a care.
The octopus paints with colors bright,
While the clams just close up tight.

Song of the Gentle Stream

A brook sings songs of silly tales,
With rocks as bouncers in wet pails.
The trout perform a flashy show,
While otters slide down high and low.

Each splash resonates like a loud cheer,
As frogs karaoke without fear.
The pebbles giggle, roll around,
While turtles just look rather profound.

Murmurs of Liquid Dreams

A gurgling brook holds whispers sweet,
That tickle feet with dancing beat.
The minnows swim with goofy grins,
Plotting pranks, as mischief begins.

The wise old rocks just sit and stare,
At fish who prank without a care.
And as the sun dips low and bright,
They jest and jive until the night.

Reflections on a Liquid Canvas

Ripples giggle in the sun,
Fish wear hats, oh what fun!
Marshmallows drift on the blue,
They toast themselves, just for you.

A duck in shades struts with flair,
While jellybeans float in the air.
Artists come with paintbrushes bright,
To color the waves with delight.

A turtle jokes, racing a breeze,
While snail serenades upon trees.
This canvas of liquid, wild and free,
Is a masterpiece for you and me.

But watch your step on the slippery bank,
Or into the drink, you'll give a prank!
So come for a laugh, splash with glee,
In this funny pool of mirth and spree.

The Dance of Waves

Waves wobble and twist like a clown,
They bounce and boogie, up and down.
Seagulls join in, on a cheat sheet,
Doing the limbo, oh so neat!

A crab does the cha-cha, sideways it glides,
While beach balls roll in slippery rides.
The sun throws confetti, oh what a sight,
As splashes of laughter paint the daylight.

Mermaids giggle with frothy hair,
They weave a necklace made of air.
The ocean hums a quirky tune,
As fish can-can 'neath the smiling moon.

Join the parade on this liquid stage,
Where everyone's silliness turns the page.
Just dip your toes, let your worries sway,
In this comical dance, sail away!

Silent Streams of Thought

A brook chuckles soft, never shy,
Whispers of secrets as ducks stroll by.
Pebbles gossip, but no one can hear,
As the bubbles chuckle, full of cheer.

An otter floats with a big wide grin,
While dreaming of fish and a cheeky spin.
Willow trees nod, joining the fun,
As shadows play, soaking up the sun.

A frog croaks jokes in a moonlit pond,
While lilies twirl and softly respond.
The stream sneezes, a spray that delights,
Sending ripples of laughter into the nights.

So sit by the bank, let your mind roam,
In the quiet giggles, find a new home.
Thoughts run deeper than the giggling brook,
In silent streams, there's more than a book.

Secrets of Serenity

In the stillness, the frogs hold court,
With croaks so loud, they'd make you snort.
A fish swims by, wearing a frown,
Claiming the flies have shut him down.

The ducks gather round, planning mischief,
Stealing breadcrumbs like it's their chief.
But watch out for that sneaky old cat,
Who dreams of a feast but ends up flat.

Stones Beneath the Surface

Pebbles laugh as waves roll near,
Making jokes we cannot hear.
A clam in shells wishes to rhyme,
Says, 'I couldn't find a shell in time!'

Snails slip-slide with snailish glee,
"Race you to that leaf!" one hollers free.
But a turtle grins, slow and steady,
Knows in the end he'll be more heady.

Cascade of Whispers

A stream gurgles, telling tales,
Of tippy-toed fish with wiggly scales.
But a log, with a grin, pipes up with cheer,
'You all should see how I float down here!'

The paddles of kayaks dance like fools,
Making waves and splashing pools.
The squirrels dive in for a quick swim,
Only to find they've forgotten how to brim!

Melodies of the Moat

In a moat, a mischievous jest,
Where frogs take turns in their quarreling quest.
"Jump far, jump high, who will be king?"
Hopping around like it's a spring fling!

A dragonfly spins tales of flight,
"Last week I danced with a candlelight!"
But the goldfish snickers, half in a trance,
"Just don't forget to avoid the plant's lance!"

Underwater Dreams

Bubbles dance in glee,
As fishes play hide and seek,
Seaweed sways with flair,
While crabs perform a cheeky peek.

A dolphin honks with joy,
Waving to a passing boat,
Mermaids giggle nearby,
As they start to float.

Octopuses tell jokes,
With arms tangled like a mess,
The clownfish chuckles loud,
In their aquatic dress.

A turtle takes a nap,
Snoring like a rusty fan,
While starfish spin around,
In their funky disco plan.

The Silence Beneath

A fish yawns wide and bright,
Perhaps it dreams of cheese,
The sea's a hidden stage,
Where laughter flows with ease.

Crabs tell tall tales of woe,
About the lost fish fry,
While seahorses dance round,
With a wink and flirty sigh.

A whale sings a low tune,
Made of bubbles and hugs,
Creating underwater memes,
It's a world full of shrugs.

Eels make jokes on the sly,
With zany zaps quite absurd,
While snails take the prize,
For slowest vines heard.

Whirling Streams of Thought

In currents wrapped in laughs,
Ideas swirl like fish,
A guppy floats on by,
Wishing for a big, bold dish.

Waves talk to the sand,
With gossip quite profound,
While terns do aerial tricks,
And land without a sound.

Jellyfish with funny hats,
Float by with great parade,
Wondering who put them there,
In this quirky charade.

A wave spills out a joke,
About the tides' big plans,
While shells roll their eyes,
And throw up their little hands.

Liquid Reflections

Mirrors in the deep,
Making faces with a splash,
A fish grimaces wide,
At his own watery bash.

Bubble winks and grins,
Share secrets from below,
While turtles dressed in style,
Float by in vibrant flow.

Anemones pull classic pranks,
Their tentacles all a-tangle,
While dolphins charge with glee,
In their high-finned jangle.

The shimmering surface laughs,
As the sun sets on this scene,
The ocean cracks a smile,
In its playful routine.

Oceanic Reverie

Waves giggle, splashing feet,
Crabs dance a sandy jig,
Seagulls squawk with cheeky flair,
Under the sun, nothing's too big.

Fish play tag beneath the tide,
While starfish wrinkle with delight,
Octopuses juggle shells with glee,
In the splashy sea, all is bright.

Surfers ride on frothy curls,
While dolphins wave and flip around,
Mermaids laugh with hair so wild,
In this ocean, joy is found.

Even the seaweed starts to sway,
Wiggling like it's lost in song,
A silly scene of ocean fun,
Where everything feels right, not wrong.

Raindrop Rhapsody

Pitter-patter on the roof,
Raindrops dance in splish-splash lines,
Every droplet, a joke to tell,
Sliding down with silly signs.

Umbrellas flipping, people twirl,
As puddles become tiny pools,
Frogs croak in a comedy show,
Nature's laughter through the rules.

Kids in boots stomp with delight,
Splashing through the bubbly scenes,
Caterpillars in slick raincoats,
Living out their soggy dreams.

Raindrops twinkling against the glass,
Singing tunes of giddy streams,
Oh, what fun the sky can have,
In the silly water themes.

Nature's Quiet Dialogue

A brook babbles, 'Listen here!'
While trees giggle, swaying low,
Leaves rustle with a ticklish breeze,
Nature holds a comedy show.

Birds chirp jokes, a feathered crew,
Squirrels giggle, running wild,
Bouncing off the branches high,
In this woodland, all are styled.

The wind whispers secrets sly,
Why did the tree cross the road?
To get to the other side, of course!
Nature's chuckles can't be owed.

Mushrooms pop up like they know,
The punchline of a hidden jest,
Gnomes chuckle from behind the bark,
In this land, humor's the best.

Voices of the Lakebed

Bubbles rise from depths below,
Fish gossip in their scaly coats,
Turtles chuckle, slow but sly,
As frogs croak punchlines in their boats.

The bulrushes sway with glee,
Whispering stories old and wise,
The lake sings lullabies at night,
Under the stars, where laughter lies.

Ducklings paddle with a splash,
Making ripples of pure delight,
While the moon grins, shining wide,
On this watery scene, so bright.

Each wave a giggle, soft and free,
The lakebed echoes with laughter so true,
In this serene, funny embrace,
Nature's joy is always anew.

Tides That Tell Forgotten Tales

In a puddle by the street,
Frogs debate who's got the beat.
They leap and croak, a silly show,
As raindrops giggle in a row.

The river swirls with tales of old,
Of fish that danced, or so I'm told.
They parade in dreams, a splashy spree,
With worms on strings, and fish tea parties!

Beneath the Boisterous Flow

Beneath the waves, the seaweed sways,
An octopus plays hide and gaze.
With eight long arms, it plays charades,
Announcing pranks in splashy braids.

A crab in a hat, quite a sight,
Tells jokes that make the dolphins light.
With bubbles popping, laughter grows,
As seahorses giggle in rows.

Tides of Solitude

The shoreline smiles with sandy glee,
A starfish jokes, 'Come fish with me!'
While clams tell tales of buried loot,
And laugh at seagulls' awkward scoot.

A wave waves back with playful grace,
While shells gossip, a clattering race.
They whisper secrets of tides alone,
Making memories out of foam.

Soft Currents of Memory

In a creek, a duck has lost its quack,
While turtles swim in a train-like pack.
They reminisce about the days,
Of sliding down the muddy bays.

Leaves float down like gossip breeze,
And frogs giggle under the trees.
With whispers soft, the waters play,
Crafting stories that drift away.

Serenity in Every Wave

The ocean giggles with a splash,
Crabs dance around in quite a dash.
Seagulls caw, they think they're grand,
While fish just chuckle, ain't life so bland?

A duck in shades floats by, all chill,
While waves make jokes, if you will.
A beach ball bounces, full of glee,
As sandy toes tickle, oh so free!

With sea foam whip, laughter writes,
As kids chase waves, enjoying sights.
The sun reads scripts, its rays do glow,
Each ripple sings, "Life's quite a show!"

So lean back, let the tides sway,
And join in the fun, don't delay.
For laughter's tide will never wane,
In this sea of joy, no room for pain.

Beyond the Shore

Far past the surf, where silliness reigns,
Starfish play tag, while jellyfish trains.
A whale tells jokes, but nobody hears,
His bellyache laughs, and brings happy tears.

The sand's a comedian, with grains that jest,
That stick to your toes, an uninvited guest.
Shells act all shy, but inside they smile,
As crabs crack jokes, all in good style.

Seashells gossip, with secrets to tell,
While the tide rolls in, and starts to yell.
An octopus winks, with eight arms in play,
"Grab a surfboard, come ride this wave today!"

With laughter afloat, it's a splashy affair,
The ocean's a stage, without a care.
So dive into fun, and let laughter soar,
Life's funny here, beyond the shore.

Secrets of Stillness

A pond sits quietly, full of surprise,
Where frogs wear hats, and fireflies rise.
They hold a ball, with lily pads round,
And giggles escape, with no one around.

The turtles are jesters, moving so slow,
While fish choreograph a splashy show.
"Who can stay still?" the dragonflies tease,
As they zip by with the greatest of ease.

The reeds break into song, it's quite a delight,
As the ripples dance in the pale moonlight.
A mouse joins in, with a tiny top hat,
Claiming it's time for a fancy pat!

With whispers so soft, the night gently calls,
To join in the fun, as stillness enthralls.
For in this calm, there's laughter untold,
A secret of joy, forever unfolds.

The Language of Streams

In the brook's babble lies a humorous spell,
Where stones laugh quietly and frogs all yell.
A squirrel takes notes, perched up on a limb,
While fish share stories of life on a whim.

The water chuckles, it giggles and flows,
With ripples that dance, like a river that knows.
"Have you heard?" says the pebble, "It's quite the fun!
Last week I met a fish who thought he could run!"

A splash of a splash, and the otters slide,
With a plop and a pop they glide side by side.
The moss is all giggly, as sunshine beams,
While the current conspired to fulfill their dreams.

So listen closely to the bubbling stream,
A language of laughter, it perfectly schemes.
In every brook, there's joy to redeem,
As life flows swiftly, like a funny dream.

Cascade of Memories

A splash of laughter, waves of cheer,
Old fish tales told, you just can't hear.
Dancing droplets, jumping high,
Together we laugh, the gulls fly by.

Bobbling thoughts in a frothy brew,
Did the fish just wink, or is it just you?
Caught in a net, where's the bait?
Tales of mischief that we narrate.

Flowing Conversations

Gurgling gossip, secrets spill,
A bobbing cork, in for the thrill.
With flowing chatter, we bob and weave,
Making waves, as we believe.

"Did you hear the water's prank?"
The fish all giggle, without a tank.
Drifting dreams on a shimm'ring flow,
Laughter cascades, it's quite the show.

A Symphony of Streams

A trio of frogs croak in tune,
Bouncing beats under the moon.
They ribbit a rhythm, don't miss a beat,
'Splish' and 'splash', oh what a feat!

With melodies brewed from bubbling springs,
Even the rocks join in and sing.
The water's a stage, a show so grand,
Fish in tuxedos, they waltz on land.

Depths of Silence

Beneath the calm, a bubble pops,
What a surprise, the laughter drops.
A fishy smirk in the deep abyss,
Who knew silence could be such bliss?

In the stillness, a tickle floats,
"Did you fart?" says the trout, then she gloats.
Giggling echoes through watery trails,
Bringing all memories, like sailing sails.

Melodies of the Mist

In the fog, a frog sings tunes,
While a fish plays a few marooned loons.
A turtle tries to do the jig,
But slips on seaweed, oh so big!

Bubbles pop like funny balloons,
As they float beneath silver moons.
A splash, a laugh, it's all so grand,
Nature's band gives us a hand!

The river dances, a silly spree,
With ducks who quack in harmony.
They waddle, they wiggle, what a sight,
Making ripples, pure delight!

A drippy drop does a little loop,
Joining the fun with a playful whoop.
Each giggle echoes through the streams,
Making light of our wildest dreams!

Harmonies of the Lake

In the calm, a raccoon hums,
While a beaver softly drums.
The fish flip-flop, dance in glee,
And frogs just croak their jubilee!

A duck in shades struts with flair,
While turtles sunbathe without a care.
A splash here, a giggle there,
They keep the mood light, full of air!

Raindrops fall, a tap-tap beat,
As squirrels join in, oh what a treat!
They twirl and spin, oh how they play,
Inventing games, come what may!

A fish throws a party, and all attend,
With snacks of lily pads, they munch and blend.
As the sun sets, they wave goodbye,
Cascading laughter still floats by!

Submerged Echoes

Beneath the waves, oh what a sight,
A crab plays peek-a-boo with delight.
The seaweed sways, on a whim,
The ocean giggles, on a whim!

A jellyfish dances, twirls in grace,
While clowns of the sea start their race.
The dolphins leap and spin around,
In this underwater playground found!

An octopus offers a game of charades,
With eight arms flailing, he never fades.
The eels groan with laughter all around,
While bubbles rise up, no sound profound!

Seahorses twirl, in jackets of glee,
Sinking and swimming, so wild and free.
As laughter rings through the coral trees,
It's a party under, with playful ease!

Flowing Thoughts

A river runs with chatty streams,
Where rocks are jesters, cracking beams.
A sailboat waves, oh what a cheer,
While sunbeams giggle, drawing near!

A worm in a boat dreams high and low,
Wishing and wishing to drift and flow.
The ripples ripple, they tease and play,
As frogs tell stories in a funny way!

The clouds above burst, raining jests,
Splashing the ground, hosting mishaps fest.
A squirrel slips on a slick, wet log,
And lands with a splash, just like a frog!

With every turn, a new surprise,
Nature's humor wears no disguise.
Laughter flows through the stream's embrace,
In this merry, wet, whimsical place!

Chronicles of the Estuary

In the estuary, pelicans dive,
Fish offer jokes, keeping dreams alive.
A turtle wears shades, a cool old chap,
While crabs throw parties with a snappy clap.

The waves are gossiping, playful and bright,
'What's the latest scandal? Is it day or night?'
The reeds are laughing, swaying with glee,
As frogs compose tunes, oh what a spree!

An otter slips by, a gourmet delight,
Stealing a sandwich—I hope it's alright!
But the seagulls just chuckle, no room for grudge,
They're too busy stealing food—oh, what a judge!

Under the sun, the estuary sparkles,
Mollusks recite jokes which always tickle.
The tide rolls in, with a wink and a wave,
In this funny realm, there's nothing to save!

Secrets in the Springs

In the springs where the bubbles pop,
Fish wear funky hats, dancing nonstop.
A frog sings off-key, but who even cares?
The dragonflies giggle, weaving through airs.

A squirrel on a branch, with a wisecrack to share,
Says, 'Ever seen a fish with a comb in its hair?'
The turtles chuckle, they've heard it before,
It's a classic old joke, by the spring's swaying door!

Barefoot children splash, making quite a mess,
While the water nymphs laugh, 'Oh what duress!'
They quench their thirst with a bubbly cheer,
In this land of secrets, the fun's crystal clear!

As the sun dips low, hues start to blend,
The springs hum a tune, where laughter won't end.
A warm breeze flows, with whispers that cling,
In this watery world, we dance and sing!

Waves of Longing

The waves play tag, oh what a sight,
Chasing each other, in pure delight.
A crab takes a selfie, all decked in sand,
While dolphins form lines, a conga band!

Seagulls squawk jokes, like stand-up stars,
'Why don't fish share? They're just shy, from afar!'
The tide roars back, with a witty retort,
'You'd laugh too loud with me if you'd trot!'

Parents build castles, but kids throw them down,
While the tide just giggles, 'You'll come back around!'
The wind sends a message, carried on high,
'Life's just a chuckle, give it a try!'

As night falls gently, waves still play coy,
Flashes of laughter will surely deploy.
The ocean, a jokester, with tides full of charm,
Leaves us all giggling without cause for alarm!

Tranquil Reflections

In calm waters where reflections lay,
A fish spins tales of a wild fray.
'You wouldn't believe the line I tried!
It was the biggest catch—but the story just died!'

The lilies roll on, twirling with glee,
While frogs leap in rhythm, can't you see?
They croak out a tune about lily pad dreams,
Dancing together in bright sunny beams.

Even the stones are chuckling along,
With echos of laughter in every song.
'Why sit so still?' a pebble will cry,
'Let's all tumble around, cartwheel and fly!'

As day fades away, the surface is bright,
With stars ricocheting, glowing at night.
A peaceful splash followed by a chuckle divine,
In tranquil reflections, the joy intertwines!

Gentle Crests

A wave just told a joke, it's true,
It splashed the shore in a playful hue.
Seagulls giggled, they took a dive,
   Chasing bubbles, so much alive.

The sunbeams danced upon the sea,
As fish wore hats, how could that be?
They swam in circles, silly and round,
   Making laughter, what a sound!

A crab tried to dance, but tripped on a shell,
Fell back in the foam with a hilarious yell.
Some seaweed tangled around its leg,
   Wiggled and jiggled, quite the peg!

So listen close to the tides' delight,
They've got stories that sparkle and bite.
With each gentle wave, there's fun to gain,
Just watch the scenes where laughter reigns.

Dreaming with the Tide

The tide is rolling with a giggle at dawn,
Carrying dreams like a sweet little fawn.
It tickles the rocks, gives them a cheer,
   Whispers of wishes, all drawing near.

Fish wear pajamas, what a sight to see,
One even claimed, "I'm as cozy as can be!"
Shells are chatting, sharing their tales,
While jellyfish dance in their flowing veils.

A dolphin appears, doing tricks in the foam,
Says, "Join the fun! There's room for your home!"
The seaweed sways to a rhythm so fine,
   Under the sun, it's a joke divine.

With tints of laughter on waves all around,
Each splash is a giggle, a joy so profound.
We dream and we laugh as we drift with the tide,
In the album of life, let fun be your guide!

Beneath the Flow

Beneath the surface, a party's awake,
With fish debating on which path to take.
They wore tiny hats, feathers and bows,
Slipping and sliding, in splendid shows.

A wise octopus shares a tall tale,
About a crab who swam heavy like a whale!
With ink for laughs, he paints the scene,
As bubbles rise up, all sparkly and keen.

Starfish chimed in with a glittery wink,
"Under the tide, we all love to think!"
Seahorses giggled, they spun in delight,
Making swirls and twirls, oh what a sight!

So if you wander where currents play,
Just remember to smile and dance, they say.
The secrets of depths are full of surprise,
With laughter unleashed, where joy never lies.

Drifting Thoughts

Drifting along, thoughts twist and glide,
Like fish caught in giggles, all hidden inside.
They ponder the clouds, so fluffy and bright,
While waves keep on laughing, oh what a sight!

A floating log joins in with a grin,
"I'm the captain now, let the fun begin!"
Leaves dance along, tossing in waves,
As turtles roll over, oh how it saves!

Drifting and dreaming, the sea plays its tune,
Whispers to shells 'neath the glowing moon.
With echoes of chuckles in salty saloon,
Even the stars in the sky hum a tune.

So let your thoughts float, your worries unchain,
In this ocean so vast, let joy be your gain.
For beneath the waves and above in the sky,
Every echo of laughter is a reason to fly.

Secrets in the Tides

The ocean has its secrets, you see,
Jellyfish gossip, wild and free.
Starfish like to tell bad jokes,
While crabs dance around like silly folks.

Waves come in like a playful friend,
Splashing on shores, they twist and bend.
Seagulls squawk with curious tones,
While seaweed winks at big, old stones.

At low tide, shells have stories to share,
About the fish with wild, frizzy hair.
Every bubble pops, a giggle escapes,
Nature's laughter in frothy drapes.

So next time you stroll by the beach,
Listen closely, let the tide teach.
Nature's humor, a precious delight,
A watery world that's ever so bright.

Harmony of Flowing Currents

Rivers chat as they twist and turn,
With funny tales, they laugh and churn.
Fish in the stream wear goofy grins,
While frogs croak jokes, nobody wins!

A beaver on lunch break bites at a twig,
Building a dam, he's dancing a jig.
The current flows, like jokes on the air,
Bringing good laughs to the land everywhere.

Worms wiggle to the rhythm of splash,
As turtles in shells try to make a dash.
The rocks chuckle under the sun,
Saying "Life's a stream, let's have some fun!"

So join in the giggles of the flowing streams,
Where nature's comedy fills our dreams.
Water's song, a playful tune,
Making us smile from morning to moon.

Lullabies of the Lake

At sunset, the lake hums a sweet song,
As ducks waddle by, not a care for wrong.
With splashes and flaps, a slippery show,
Happy beavers say, "Go with the flow!"

Fish jump high, hoping for treats,
While lily pads dance to secret beats.
The frogs start to croak, a comedic choir,
Their love for the stage never seems to tire.

Wind whispers tales of laughter and glee,
Tickling the waves, wild and free.
Even the otters slide with delight,
Joking around till the end of the night.

So listen close to the lake's gentle sighs,
Mirroring laughter beneath the skies.
Where the water sings its soft lullaby,
With a sprinkle of giggles, oh my, oh my!

Dances on the Shimmering Shore

On the shore, the sand has a flow,
Where crabs hustle as melodious shows.
Shells spin tales of days gone by,
While seagulls and dolphins wink and sigh.

Each wave that rushes brings a chuckle,
As children dig holes, causing a tussle.
They splash and dash in a wild parade,
Nature's stage for a grand charade.

The sun dips low, painting skies aglow,
As starfish embrace the ebb and flow.
Time for laughter, let spirits soar,
As whispers of fun lead to encore.

So dance with the tide, let your heart soar,
Join in the jest on the sandy floor.
A world of giggles, bright and pure,
At the shimmering shore, there's always a cure!

Beneath the Glassy Surface

Bubbles tickle as fish parade,
A crab is dancing, unafraid.
With seaweed wigs, they strut about,
The ocean's got a spunky clout.

Starfish boast of sunlit days,
While otters giggle, in playful ways.
"Catch me," they say, "if you can!"
A splash and dash, banter's the plan.

Jellyfish float, a gooey show,
They bob and weave, putting on a glow.
"Did you hear the one about a clam?"
"Oh please, not that old jam!"

The tide ticks off with a cheeky smirk,
While seagulls gossip and do their work.
The ocean's mirth bubbles like foam,
With laughter echoing, it feels like home.

Remembering Under the Waves

An octopus recalls a date,
With a dolphin—oh, how great!
"Did he bring flowers made of kelp?
Or was it more of an awkward yelp?"

Turtles reminisce about races lost,
While squids write novels at no cost.
"Once I tripped on a floating log,"
"Epic fail," said the seaweed frog.

Seashells gossip of visitors bold,
"Last year's tide was quite the gold!"
Fish swap tales of their wild chase,
"Remember that time—the big wave's face?"

The current hums a tune so sweet,
As crabs jive in a funky beat.
Beneath the waves, laughter flows,
In the depths, speculation grows.

Tales from the Rippled Edge

At the shore, a clumsy seal,
"Watch me now," he spins the wheel!
With a splash, he steals the scene,
And surfboards laugh at the routine.

"Did you hear what that whale said?
He dreamt of skies, but stayed in bed!"
Turtledoves dive for the punchline,
While crab juggling becomes divine.

"Seagulls prefer fries by the bay,
Thieves at best, they steal the day!"
With waves hosting a giggling spree,
It's a beach party, bested by glee.

Underneath the sun's warm gaze,
Every ripple spins its maze.
From sandy shores to waters deep,
The laughter echoes—there's joy to reap.

Conversations with the Ocean's Heart

The ocean winks with glistening trails,
"Tell me your secrets, oh windy gales!"
A whale's been gossiping wide and far,
"Amongst the currents, I'm quite the star!"

Starfish insist they're fashion-forward,
"Check my new hue! Aren't you floored?"
The coral snickers with vibrant hues,
"Only the brave can wear these shoes!"

Sea turtles debate on which path to choose,
"Shall we cruise the tide or sing the blues?"
The pelicans flap in a comical chase,
In the aquatic realm, laughter's the grace.

From barnacles clinging with hearty zest,
"Life's quite funny when you're at your best!"
Beneath this lens, friendship flows free,
In a world of waves, joy's the decree.

Voices of the Wavering Waters

The stream sings tunes that sound like a joke,
Fish gather 'round for a slip-slap poke.
A duck quacks out punchlines, a true giggle treat,
As frogs join the chorus with a ribbiting beat.

Bubbles burst laughter, swirling with glee,
Each ripple a chuckle from the roots of a tree.
Turtles in sunglasses, all chill on a rock,
Give the fish a wink, oh what a shock!

Tiny boats made of leaves, they drift and they sway,
Getting caught in the giggles of this watery play.
The sandcastles laugh, they crack up and fall,
Who knew that the puddles could have such a ball?

At dusk they still jam, a finned party alive,
While crickets compose, the whole marsh takes a dive.
A night by the bank, full of jokes and delight,
In this silly small world, everything feels right.

Reflections of a Moonlit Lagoon

The moon grins down, it's a sight to behold,
While crabs do the cha-cha on sand so bold.
Fish flaunt their scales, a glittery sight,
As the tide brings the laughter, all through the night.

Stars twinkle like bubbles that just want to pop,
With jellyfish swinging, they never will stop.
A sea turtle breaks dance on a wobbly shell,
While oysters all giggle, they're under a spell.

The night air is buzzing, a humorous tease,
As waves whisper secrets on a gentle breeze.
Seagulls are swooping, oh, what a display,
Trading jokes with the dolphins in their own wacky way!

With a splash and a laugh, the lagoon's a delight,
Where each playful creature joins in through the night.
Beneath a big spotlight, the moon stays in check,
In this lagoon party, it's a real love fest!

Tranquil Streams of Thought

Thoughts flow like water, they tumble and glide,
With pebbles as punchlines, they never can hide.
A squirrel waterskiing, it's quite the odd sight,
While the otters play tag in the soft morning light.

Each ripple's a giggle, a wave full of cheer,
As frogs play hopscotch with no hint of fear.
Leaves drift downstream, they laugh as they pass,
Creating a whirlpool of absurd looking class.

The breeze has a tickle, it's whispering jokes,
And the trees start to rustle as if they are folks.
With warriors of bubbles, the fish start to duel,
In the river's grand theater, absurd is the rule.

Together they dance in a swirling, wild spree,
With laughter and fun in this fun, flowing sea.
A world full of chuckles, so colorful, bright,
In the streams of our thoughts, where all feels just right.

Cascades of Hidden Stories

The waterfall chatters, it rumbles and spins,
While frogs offer monologues with silly grins.
Each splash is a riddle, a story to share,
As squirrels giggle loudly, without a care.

The rocks hold legends, they whisper and roar,
Of turtles in top hats that dance on the shore.
With creeks full of giggles, the fish play charades,
While the crickets and cicadas hum sweet serenades.

A beaver's a judge, with a wooden gavel,
While dragonflies zoom in a wild, happy travel.
The mossy green banks hold secrets of jest,
In this cascade of tales, we are truly blessed.

So come hear the stories, where laughter runs free,
In this splashy delight, join the mirthful spree.
Nature's own humor, it flows without end,
In these cascades of tales, let the fun never bend!

Serenity in a Ripple

A fish with a hat swims by me,
It nods and winks quite hilariously.
Bubbles dance like they know a joke,
While lily pads wear a leafy cloak.

The frogs croak a tune, it's quite absurd,
They sing with a flair, they're quite the nerds.
Each ripple laughs, a giggly sound,
As turtles twist in joy, unbound.

The sun gives a grin, what a sight,
Spreading warmth, oh what delight!
It's as if nature's one big jest,
In this giggly realm, I'm feeling blessed.

With each wave's flick, a playful cheer,
The pond's our stage, come gather near!
In silliness, we find our way,
As every splash invites to play!

Chasing the Cascades

A waterfall's tantrum, oh what a splash!
It tumbles and rumbles with a boisterous crash.
Fish flopping about, trying to leap,
Bumping their heads, not one can keep.

The rocks grumble back, 'You're too clumsy!'
As the water roars, all feeling fumbly.
A squirrel takes a dive—oh what a sight!
He swims fast, thinking he's quite bright.

With each drop down, the giggles grow,
As everything dances, together in flow.
Little ducks quack, "Let's start a race!"
And tumble right down, it's quite the chase!

The splash zone's alive, full of cheer,
While water sprites laugh, "Water's our beer!"
So let's ride the rapids, sing loud and clear,
In this cascade of fun, let's have no fear!

Songs from the Abyss

Down in the depths where sunlight's shy,
Octopuses play hide and seek, oh my!
With every flip, they change their hue,
Singing ballads like a old blues crew.

A crab joins in with a tap-tap beat,
While anglerfish strut with a flashy seat.
Eels coil and twist in the tune's warm hug,
The sea's a dance floor, pull up a slug!

Mermaids laugh as they swing by,
Dropping pearls with a wink and a sigh.
"Join us, dear friend! Don't you feel free?
In this salty giggle, come dance with me!"

With bubbles as maracas, seaweed sways,
Underwater raves filled with playful displays.
The anchor of joy, forever persists,
In the depths of the sea, where laughter twists.

The Calm Before the Wave

Before the storm, the sea lies still,
The crabs start plotting from the hill.
"Let's hide the salt!" one scuttles around,
As the gulls prepare to make a sound.

A starfish takes a nap, dreaming of pies,
While seashells gossip with clouded eyes.
"Do you hear that rumble?" a clam asks shy,
It's just the ocean letting out its sigh.

The clouds wear frowns, a gray, grumpy team,
While shimmer-fish dance in a peaceful dream.
"Quick! Grab your floaties!" the waves seem to say,
As we all await the splashy buffet!

But here comes the tide, a mischievous tease,
With giggly splashes that dance with ease.
"Surprise!" it shouts, with a watery grin,
And we laugh and tumble, let the fun begin!

Voices of the Tides

The waves are chatting, quite a clatter,
Seagulls swoop in, causing a matter.
They're gossiping fish with scales that gleam,
While crabs tell tales, or so it may seem.

A starfish giggles, stuck on a rock,
It tickles the seaweed, what a funny shock!
Bubbles rise up and burst with a splash,
While droll dolphins start a splashy bash.

Shells hold secrets with giggly grins,
As shrimp do the cha-cha, wiggling fins.
A sea cucumber jokes in a slow-paced dance,
While plankton twirl in a whimsical trance.

So listen closely, to the ocean's jest,
Where laughter and joy put the waves to the test.
In this salty circus, with all the delights,
The tides keep laughing into the nights.

Beneath the Moonlit Surface

Under the moon, a fish takes a dive,
It spins and twirls, feeling alive.
They slip and slide on a watery floor,
A school of sardines, a funny decor.

The jellyfish wobble, with a giggle or two,
As clowns of the sea, in a shimmering hue.
They dance in the light, like a glowing show,
While octopuses juggle, stealing the glow.

Crabs in tuxedos, with top hats on tight,
Strut 'round the reef in quite a delight.
They wave at the sharks, who roll their eyes,
And conch shells laugh, what a surprise!

With moonlight above and laughter within,
It's a silly affair beneath ocean's skin.
In this watery world, where fun's always near,
The depths hold humor, not a hint of fear.

Drifting with the Current

Floating along, a fish tells a joke,
As the current swirls, it gives a poke.
A sea turtle chuckles, takes his sweet time,
Saying, 'Slow and steady wins the prime.'

A starry night, with starfish in tow,
They throw a party, not moving too slow.
They sip on the sea foam, giggling with glee,
Reef parties are wild, come join the spree!

With each gentle wave, the laughter comes clear,
As minnows burst forth, filled with good cheer.
The coral shrieks jokes, painted in hues,
While clowns wait in line for the best sea views.

So drift with the tides, let the currents decide,
Join the funny fish in their cosmic glide.
With each little ripple and wave on the brink,
They'll keep you smiling, quicker than you think!

Whispers of the Ocean's Veil

Voices arise from the depths, oh my,
A clam's got a secret, let's not be shy.
It whispers to shells, in a deep, hushed tone,
While crabby comedians prank on their own.

The tides are ticklish, they bubble and squeak,
As fish tell tales of the sea's sneaky streak.
A playful dolphin rolls, makes a big splash,
While sardines giggle and break out in thrash.

In this underwater world, nothing's so grave,
The humor flows free, like a rippling wave.
With each gentle swish, the tales come alive,
As bubbles of laughter around them will thrive.

So listen close to the waves' gentle call,
The ocean's a jest, come one, come all.
In the depths and the bubbles, mirth bubbles free,
Making sure each tide is filled with glee.

Beneath the Aquamarine Veil

Beneath the waves, fish dance and prance,
With bubbles popping, they twirl in a trance.
A clam with a hat gives advice very wise,
"Don't trust the octopus who wears a disguise!"

Seaweed waltzes, a slippery show,
While crabs throw a party and go toe-to-toe.
The jellyfish giggle, all jiggly and bright,
As sardines form conga lines, what a sight!

A dolphin arrives with a spirit so grand,
"Let's surf the waves!" he shouts, raising a fin-hand.
But the seahorse struggles, he's had quite a day,
"I'm too small for this, give my rider away!"

A guppy's bold trick sets the fish all a-laugh,
He sneezes a bubble that turns into half!
"Oops, wrong direction! Watch out for my splash!"
The tides carry secrets with a bubbly crash!

Whispers from the Depths

In the deep blue, the eels play peek,
With squiggly tails, they wiggle and squeak.
"Have you heard the joke about a fish in a net?"
"He said, 'I'm hooked!' and that was his fret!"

The grouper grins wide, his scales all a-glint,
"Why don't fish play piano? They just can't find the splint!"
And starfish roll over, they laugh on the floor,
"At least we do not have to deal with the shore!"

Anemones sway, tossing jokes to the tune,
While clowns in the coral put on a cartoon.
"Why did the sea turtle cross the lagoon?"
"To get to the shell station before the big monsoon!"

Laughter bubbles up like a frothy cascade,
With scales and fins, they spin in a parade.
The laughter of creatures from deep down below,
Sends ripples of joy, just watch how they glow!

Cascade of Silken Secrets

From currents that twist, secrets rise with a swish,
A fish in a bowtie fulfills every wish.
He tells tales of pirates who searched for lost gold,
But ended up dancing, now that's quite bold!

A whimsical otter holds court with a wink,
He juggles sharp shells; they all start to sink.
"Not my fault!" says the crab with the fancy top hat,
"I'd be smart too if I'd sat on a mat!"

The bubbles of laughter bounce high through the stream,
As a clown fish rehearses his favorite scheme.
"Hey guys! Let's dive under the seaweed!" he shouts,
"And scare the old crab—he's full of old doubts!"

So twist and swirl through the whimsical sea,
With laughter that dances as bright as can be.
For under the surface, things aren't as they seem,
Fish comedy's brewing beneath the moonbeam!

The Language of Flowing Liquid

When streams start to chat, listen closely, oh dear,
A fish named Carl whispers, "Aquatic career!"
He's got gills, but he dreams of singing on land,
"I'd be the next star, but who'd wave my hand?"

Bubbles collect like a giggle-filled crowd,
Eels spin their tales, feeling cheeky and proud.
"Why do fish hate playing cards with a shark?"
"Because he always jaws about going out in the dark!"

Drifting through reeds, the humor takes flight,
As turtles exchange puns, just feeling delight.
"What's a fish's favorite instrument?" they inquire,
"The bass guitar! It sets our hearts on fire!"

In this river of chuckles, let's swim and unite,
For laughter is music and fun is our flight.
So let words flow freely, let verse be our art,
With each splash and ripple, we share from the heart!

Liquid Lullabies

Silly fish in fancy hats,
Dancing under waves like acrobats.
They joke about their bubble dreams,
While splashing in their watery streams.

Bubbles burst with little pops,
Creating laughter that never stops.
The squids play cards, the crabs throw pies,
As seaweed tickles the starry skies.

Jellyfish bounce in a jelly jam,
While clowns of coral perform a scam.
With each flip, a giggle slips,
As ocean's laughter never tips.

So join the fun, leap and dive,
Where fishy tricks help us thrive.
In this pool of liquid cheer,
The waves are giggling, come and hear!

Echoes Beneath the Surface

Beneath the waves, the echoes play,
They tell of fish who lost their way.
With fins all flapping, what a sight,
They dance for joy in pure delight.

One fish claims it caught a shoe,
While others swear it's so untrue!
They bubble secrets, laugh, and tease,
As current giggles through the trees.

A dolphin sings a silly tune,
Twisting and flipping, causing a swoon.
With every splash, a chorus forms,
Reef ticket sales for ocean storms!

So listen close, take in a cheer,
The ocean's banter, loud yet dear.
In this watery realm of chats,
Laughter flows from fins and hats!

Secrets of the Deep

In the depths where shadows dance,
Bubbles giggle, giving a chance.
A crab wearing glasses reads a map,
While a fish in stripes takes a nap.

"Why did the clam cross the reef?"
It giggles softly, "To find some beef!"
Turtles snort and roll with glee,
As dolphins play hide and seek, whee!

An octopus with juggling flair,
Shows off tricks with eight to spare.
As laughter bubbles up so bright,
The secrets swim in pure delight.

So dive right in, forget your woes,
Let ocean giggles tickle your toes.
In the depths, where secrets creep,
You'll find more laughs than dreams to keep!

Murmurs of the Stream

A brook babbles with silly rhymes,
While frogs in top hats chime in times.
They croak their songs, a ribbit cheer,
   As water dances, crystal clear.

A snail, with swagger, takes it slow,
   Strolling past the catfish show.
"Why are you moving so unstylish?"
The catfish giggles, "I'm just stylish!"

   Pebbles gossip, stories unfold,
About the fish who's rich and bold.
They swish and swirl, a merry stream,
   With laughter gliding like a dream.

So pause and listen, hear them play,
   Join this watery, funny fray.
In every curve, a joke unfolds,
Where nature's giggle never grows old!

Serenity's Current

A fish in a bow tie swims with flair,
Doing the backstroke, like he just doesn't care.
His stylish swim moves make everyone gawk,
While turtles attempt their own version of talk.

The lily pads giggle, they float and they sway,
As dragonflies buzz in a comic ballet.
One leaped for a fly, but missed with a splat,
Ending up stuck in a soft sea of that.

With gurgling bubbles, the brook starts to chuckle,
The pebbles are laughing, all cuddled in huddle.
A frog bursts the bubble with a loud croak,
And all of the ripples make room for a joke.

But when the sun sets, the humor takes flight,
The twilight brings calm, oh what a delight!
For in every splash, there's a story to weave,
Of fishes in suits, who just love to believe.

Beneath the Calm

Beneath the surface, fish throw a spree,
   A party of bubbles, wild and free.
The octopus juggles with its eight arms wide,
   While seaweed sways, in its own goofy stride.

Clams snap their shells to the beat of a drum,
   While crabs do a shuffle, oh isn't it fun?
   The sea cucumbers just play it cool,
     Swaying along, they abide by the rule.

A dolphin pops up, wearing shades of bright blue,
Says, "Dive in, my friends! Join my anti-gravity crew!"
   With sea turtles spinning, they all spin around,
     As bubbles burst forth with a comical sound.

In the calm, there's chaos, you just have to look,
   Where laughter and splashes bring joy like a book.
   So join in the antics, don't be in a rush,
     For beneath the calm, there's always a hush.

Driftwood Dreams

On driftwood dreams, the otters slide,
Launching off branches, it's quite the ride!
They squeak and they laugh with each joyful jump,
As a nearby squirrel nearly takes a tumble and thump.

The logs float on rivers, with whispers and giggles,
As beavers in hats dance silly little wiggles.
They tap their big tails, the beat's in their grip,
Creating a rhythm that makes drifters flip.

With nudging and nudging, they tumble and play,
Fish think it's funny, "What a wild display!"
They cheer from below, forming bubbles so bright,
Creating a canvas of giggles and light.

As twinkling stars cast a glow on the stream,
The driftwood keeps rolling in a dreamy theme.
With laughter and joy, the night starts to gleam,
As otters and stars share a wonderful dream.

Dancers in the Rain

Raindrops arrive with a plop and a splash,
The frogs in the puddles make quite the mad dash.
They wear little boots and dance with such glee,
Each leap is a pirouette, oh can't you see?

The worms join the party, wearing slimy ties,
They wiggle and squirm, beneath gloomy skies.
With a wobble and shuffle, they dance without care,
While puddles are formed, it's a rain-soaked affair.

A snail joins the fun with a rhythmic glide,
Sliding so slick, he can't seem to hide.
While others do twirls, he just takes it slow,
You'd think he's the king of this soggy disco.

With giggles and splashes in the muddy terrain,
The critters conduct, their own quirky refrain.
So don't mind the puddles, just come join the fun,
For dancers in rain shine brighter than sun!

Fluid Conversations in Twilight

Beneath the moon's soft, silly glow,
The ripples dance, putting on a show.
"Is that a fish or just my shoe?"
The pond laughs loud, "Who knows with you!"

In twilight's chat, the frogs all croon,
Mixing up tunes with a playful tune.
One says, "Jump!" the other, "Swim!"
While minnows giggle, all on a whim!

The willows sway, with gossip to share,
"Did you see that splash? What a flair!"
Each droplet laughs, rolls on the ground,
As turtles spin tales that astound!

So come join the fun, don't be late,
The twilight's chat is quite first-rate!
With jokes and splashes, all round the lake,
It's a watery ball; make no mistake!

A Symphony of Moving Reflections

In the pond, the ducks take flight,
Their quacks compose a wobbly fright.
"Can you dance?" asks one with flair,
"Only on water!" replies in air.

Sunsets paint with colors bright,
As fish flash by, oh what a sight!
"Did you bring snacks for this fine feast?"
"Oh no, just bubbles! I'm such a beast!"

The turtles dream of races bold,
While snails, in slow, their stories told.
Each splash a note in playful song,
The rhythm's off, but we sing along!

A symphony made beneath the skies,
With chirps and croaks, oh how time flies!
"Take this tune, we'll share the laughs!"
As ripples dance in playful drafts!

Crooning of Crystalline Depths

In crystal depths, the fish all sway,
Crooning songs that drift away.
A minnow sings of pasta dreams,
"I'd trade my scales for creamy creams!"

The bubbles pop, in rhythm fine,
While barnacles hum a silly line.
"Why don't we wear hats and dance?"
"Oh please, my friend, give me a chance!"

With bright-eyed joy, the pebbles grin,
"Who knew these depths could hold such spin?"
Goldfish twirl with flippy glee,
"Next par-tay, don't forget to invite me!"

A giggling wave gives a playful shove,
"Let's throw a bash, with plenty of love!"
In depths where secrets twirl and twine,
Crooning echoes lead to laughter divine!

Secrets Held in a Currents' Gaze

In currents swirled with secrets spun,
Each ripple holds a sprinkle of fun.
A fish whispers, "What shall we explore?"
"Let's dive down deep for tales galore!"

A squirrel by the bank looks on in awe,
"Did you hear that? What a quirky law!"
As banks of moss giggle, letting us see,
The secrets we hold beneath, wild and free.

"Hey, look, a twig! I think it's a boat!"
"More like a log that's taking a coat!"
The crabs debate, in a comical race,
While turtles shrug, "At least we have space!"

In currents that shimmer and tease the day,
Laughter bubbles in a playful display.
No one knows quite how it began,
But amidst the flow, we'll all be fans!

www.ingramcontent.com/pod-product-compliance
Lightning Source LLC
Chambersburg PA
CBHW072216070526
44585CB00015B/1363